To the Teacher

SEASONS is a Learning Works mini-unit created especially for children in grades one through four. The purpose of this unit is to blend the presentation of facts about seasons with the practice of essential skills to produce the very best in theme-related teaching and results-oriented learning.

Information about seasons is presented in easy-to-read passages. Kids are told that the year is divided into four parts called seasons. Then they learn about some of the weather phenomena and natural changes that occur in each one. Associated activities involve children in observing and recording, comparing and matching, measuring and graphing, ordering and sequencing, reading and following directions, and locating and using information. These tasks are carefully designed to improve hand-eye coordination; increase skill in visual discrimination, word recognition, and spelling; stimulate curiosity; and foster creative expression.

In addition to information and activity sheets, this book contains two **All-Purpose Worksheets**, one featuring snowmen and the other picturing clouds. You can reproduce either one of these sheets, add content—weather words to be looked up, spelling words to be learned, math problems to be worked—and reproduce again so that you will have one for every member of your class.

This book also contains two pages of **Facts About Seasons and Weather**, instructions for five **Correlated Activities** suitable for small-group or whole-class projects, a **glossary** of related terms, a **Seasonally Sensitive Award**, and some **Special Awards** with which you can thank classroom helpers and recognize outstanding effort. Also, the **Clip Art** on page 48 and the many illustrations throughout this book can be reproduced and used on bulletins, games, invitations, name tags, notes, and newsletters.

This mini-unit offers stimulating activities in a seasonal context so that young learners can strengthen their skills in essential areas while becoming more aware of the natural world around them.

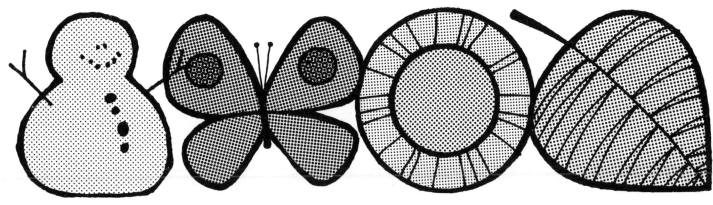

Contents

SEASONS

Written by Sherri Butterfield

Illustrated by Beverly Armstrong

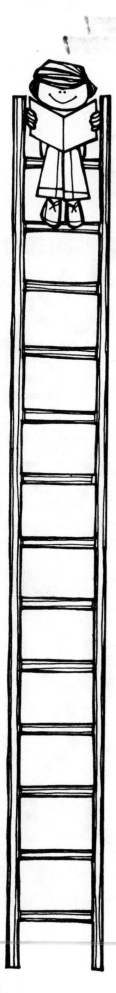

The Learning Works

The purchase of this book entitles the individual
classroom teacher to reproduce copies for use
in the classroom.

The reproduction of any part for an entire school
or school system or for commercial use is strictly
prohibited.

No form of this work may be reproduced or
transmitted or recorded without written permis-
sion from the publisher.

Write for information about our educational products.
The Learning Works • Box 6187, Dept. N • Santa Barbara, CA 93160

What Is a Season?

A year has four parts. Each part is called a **season**.
The four seasons in a year are winter, spring, summer,
and fall.

winter

spring

summer

fall

In Winter

In winter the air is cold. The trees are bare. The wind blows, and water turns to ice. Snow falls from gray skies. Heavy coats and warm fires feel good. Color this picture of winter.

Name _____

Winter Words

Look at the letters in this box. Find and circle ten words that go with winter.

```
B  O  O  T  S  N  V  D
C  O  A  T  K  O  W  E
C  J  R  C  A  P  X  F
D  M  I  T  T  E  N  S
S  N  O  W  E  R  Z  L
E  M  U  I  C  E  A  E
F  N  V  N  C  O  L  D
G  O  W  D  M  U  C  K
```

Word Box

boots • cap • coat • cold • ice
mittens • skate • sled • snow • wind

What Is Snow?

Snow is tiny white pieces of ice. When the air is very cold, water on the ground turns to ice. Water in the air freezes also. It becomes tiny white pieces of ice. We call these tiny ice pieces **crystals**. Each crystal is a snowflake.

Snowflakes are very, very small. You almost never see one snowflake alone. You usually see many snowflakes together in

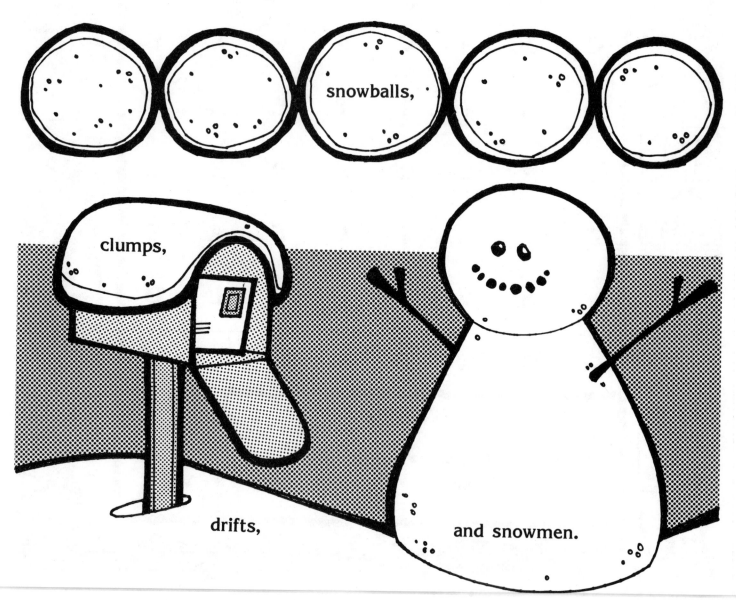

snowballs,

clumps,

drifts,

and snowmen.

Name _____

Snowflakes

Snowflakes are very special. All snowflakes have six points. Each snowflake has its own shape. Connect these numbered dots to find a snowflake shape.

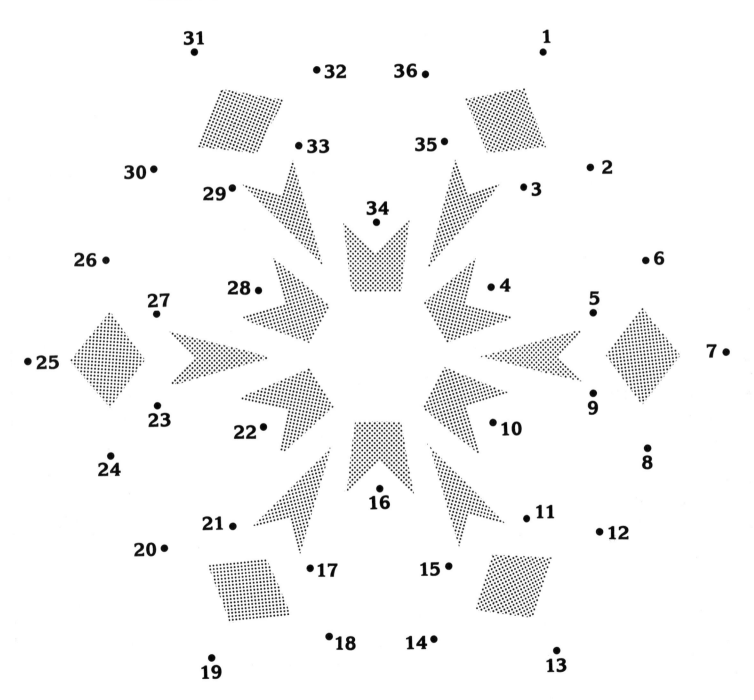

Name _____

Make a Snowflake

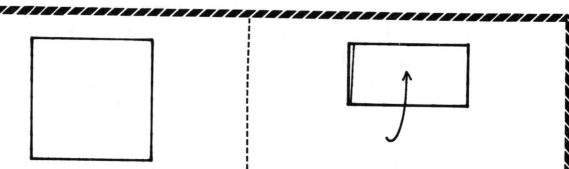

1. Cut a square of paper.

2. Fold the paper in half.

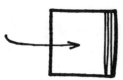

3. Fold the paper in half again.

4. Fold the paper in half again.

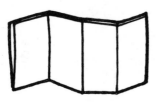

5. Open the paper this far.

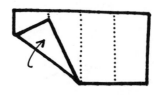

6. Fold the left side up.

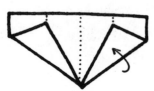

7. Fold the right side up.

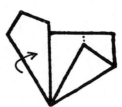

8. Fold the left side up again.

Name _____

Make a Snowflake
(continued)

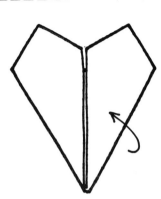

9. Fold right side up again.

10. Fold left side over right.

11. Draw a simple design.

12. Cut on the lines you have drawn.

13. Open your snowflake carefully.

14. Do it again. This time, draw a different design. Cut in different places. Make a different snowflake.

Name _____

Winter Walk

Take a winter walk in these woods. Find and color the **cap**, **coat**, **mittens**, **skates**, **skis**, and **sled** some-one has hidden there.

Name _____

All Winter Long

There are twenty-six letters in the alphabet. Some of these letters are called **vowels**. The letters **a**, **e**, **i**, **o**, and **u** are vowels. If a vowel says its name in a word, we call it a **long vowel**. The vowel **o** in the word **cold** is long. Color the pictures with long-vowel names.

cap	coat	fire
ice	mittens	scarf
skate	sled	snow

Name _____

Hot or Not?

Read the words very carefully. In each box, circle
the *one* word that goes *better* with winter.

1.	bicycle	sled
2.	coat	swimsuit
3.	cold	hot
4.	fast	fire
5.	freeze	melt
6.	ice	if
7.	picnic	popcorn
8.	dust	snow
9.	skate	sandal
10.	wade	wind

In Spring

In spring the air gets warmer. Ice and snow melt. New leaves grow on bare trees. Tiny green shoots push up through dead brown grass. Red and yellow flowers bloom. The weather does not stay the same. It changes. Sometimes the sun shines from a clear blue sky. At other times, the gray clouds gather, and it rains. Then raincoats, boots, and umbrellas help to keep us dry. Color this picture of spring.

Name _____

Spring Words

Look at the letters in this box. Find and circle
eleven words that go with spring.

```
S  U  N  D  G  R  O  W
I  M  E  L  T  N  S  A
Q  B  L  O  O  M  D  R
G  R  A  S  S  D  O  M
G  E  S  H  I  N  E  M
C  L  O  U  D  S  T  V
F  L  O  W  E  R  S  D
R  A  I  N  C  O  A  T
```

Word Box

bloom	•	clouds	•	flowers	•	grass
grow	•	melt	•	raincoat	•	shine
	sun	•	umbrella	•	warm	

What Is Weather?

Weather is how the outside air looks and feels. To tell about weather, we say how warm or cold, wet or dry, and cloudy or clear the air is. We also say how fast the wind is blowing.

sunny · partly cloudy · cloudy · rainy · stormy · windy

Name _____

Weather Watch

Watch the weather for a week. Each day, color the
picture or pictures that tell about the weather.

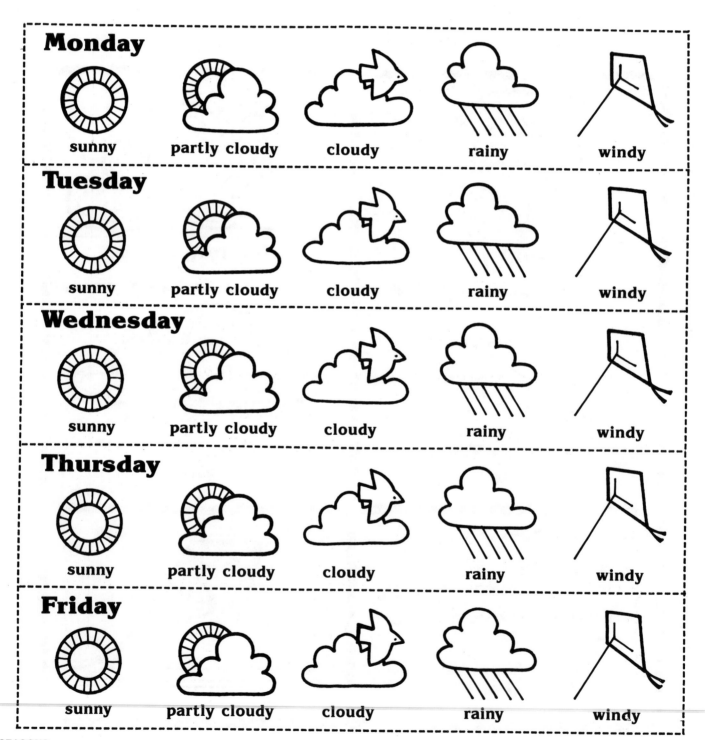

Monday
sunny   partly cloudy   cloudy   rainy   windy

Tuesday
sunny   partly cloudy   cloudy   rainy   windy

Wednesday
sunny   partly cloudy   cloudy   rainy   windy

Thursday
sunny   partly cloudy   cloudy   rainy   windy

Friday
sunny   partly cloudy   cloudy   rainy   windy

Name _____

A Month's Worth of Weather

Watch the weather for one month. Each day, tell how the outside air looks and feels by coloring a box on the Weather Watch sheet (page 18). At the end of the month, make a pictograph to show what a month's worth of weather was like.

How to Make a Pictograph

1. Get a 12-inch-by-36-inch sheet of paper.
2. Print the name of the month at the top.
3. Using a pencil and a ruler, draw lines on the paper as shown below.
4. Print the words **Sunny Days, Partly Cloudy Days, Cloudy Days**, and **Rainy Days** to name the rows.
5. Look at your **Weather Watch** sheets.

   How many **sunny day** pictures did you color? ☐

   How many **partly cloudy day** pictures did you color? ☐

   How many **cloudy day** pictures did you color? ☐

   How many **rainy day** pictures did you color? ☐

6. Count out weather pictures (from page 17) to equal the numbers you wrote in the boxes above.
7. Carefully tape or glue these pictures to your sheet of paper in rows.

Name of Month

Sunny Days	 ☼ ☼ ☼ ☼ ☼ ☼ ☼
Partly Cloudy Days	 ⛅ ⛅ ⛅ ⛅ ⛅
Cloudy Days	 ☁ ☁ ☁ ☁ ☁ ☁
Rainy Days	 🌧 🌧 🌧 🌧

What Are Clouds?

Clouds are groups of water drops or ice crystals. They seem to float in the air. Clouds come in different sizes and take many shapes.

Some clouds are thin white wisps of ice crystals. They form high above the earth where the air is very cold. These clouds are called **cirrus**.

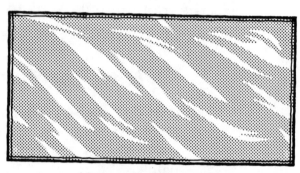

cirrus clouds

Some clouds are dark gray layers of raindrops. These clouds are called **nimbostratus**. They make drizzle and showers.

nimbostratus clouds

Some clouds are big and billowy. Alone in a blue sky, they look like white dollops of whipped cream or mashed potatoes. These clouds are called **cumulonimbus**. The air in cumulonimbus clouds is rough and windy. In groups, they produce storms with flashing lightning and crashing thunder. For this reason, they are also called **thunderheads**.

cumulonimbus clouds

Name _____

Cloud Search

Watch the sky for several days. See how many of these kinds of clouds you can find. Put an **X** in the box beside the name of each one you see.

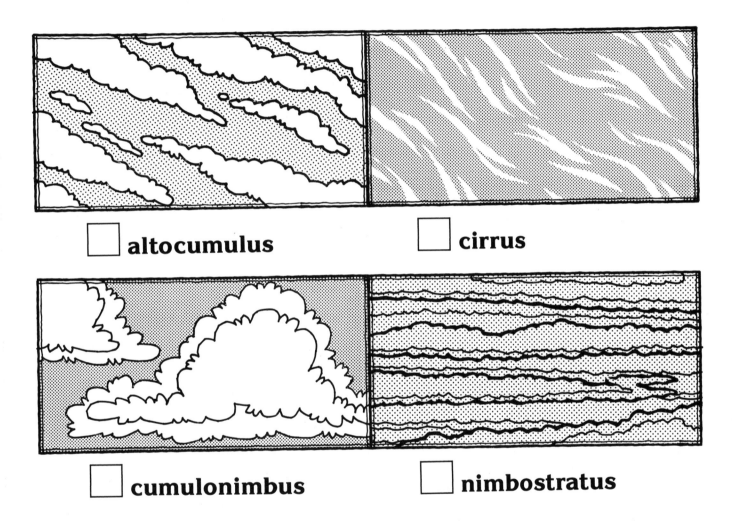

☐ **altocumulus**   ☐ **cirrus**

☐ **cumulonimbus**   ☐ **nimbostratus**

Clouds are usually white or gray. But at sunset, they turn soft pink, bright orange, pale lavender, or deep purple. Enjoy the colors of clouds at sunset. Then color these pictures.

Name _____

What Is Rain?

Rain is water falling in drops. Sometimes, the drops are tiny. They seem to float in the air. You can feel them wet and cool on your face when you walk outside. This kind of rain is called **mist**.

Sometimes, the drops are a little larger. Not much water falls, but there is enough to wet the streets and make them shine. This kind of rain is called **drizzle**.

Sometimes, the drops are large. Lots of water falls. It makes puddles on the sidewalks and turns dirt into mud. This kind of rain is called a **shower**.

Sometimes, the rain comes down in sheets. The wind blows in strong gusts. Jagged streaks of lightning cut across the sky, and thunder rumbles. This kind of rain is called a **thunderstorm**.

Write these five water words in the puzzle. Look at the letters and count the squares to see where each word fits.

drizzle • mist • rain • shower • storm

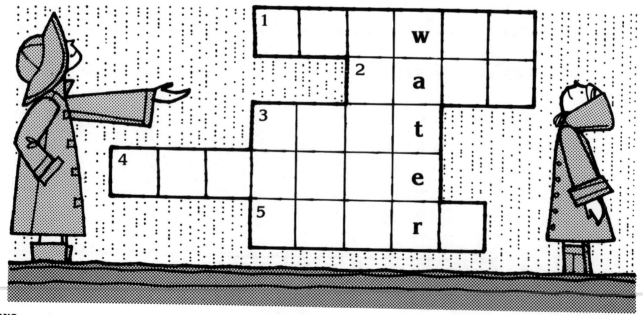

Name _____

Under an Umbrella

An **umbrella** is made by stretching paper or cloth over ribs. These ribs are hinged so that the umbrella can be opened and closed.

Umbrellas were first used long ago in China and Egypt. People in these hot lands used umbrellas to shade themselves from the sun. Later, people in England used umbrellas to keep dry during rainy weather.

To find the umbrella hidden in this picture, color it according to the color code.

Color Code

a red	**c** yellow	**e** blue	**g** brown
b orange	**d** green	**f** purple	

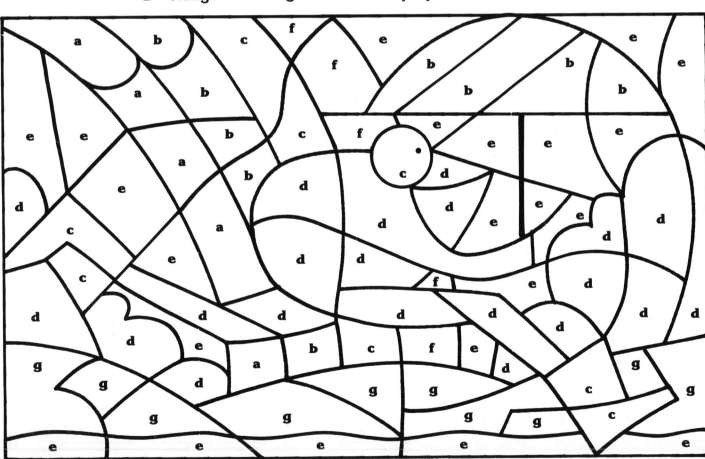

Name _____

Make a Rain Gauge

A **gauge** is an instrument used for measuring. A **rain gauge** is a special instrument used to measure the amount of water that falls during a rain. Follow these steps to make and use your own rain gauge.

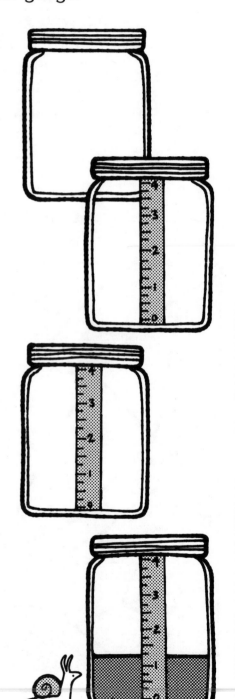

1. Get a jar with a wide mouth and straight sides. The jar you choose should be made of plastic (so it won't break) and should have an opening that is the same width as its sides. Many jelly, peanut butter, and salad dressing jars are this shape. For example, the 22-ounce Skippy peanut butter jar is ideal.

2. Place a strip of adhesive or masking tape one inch wide on the side of this jar so that it runs from the bottom to the top.

3. Using a ruler and a pen with permanent ink, mark the tape in inches.

4. Number these marks. Start at the bottom with zero and continue to the top of the tape.

5. Place one half-inch and two quarter-inch marks within each inch.

6. The next time the weather report calls for rain, set your rain gauge out in the open—away from eaves, gutters, and trees—where rain will fall directly into it.

7. When the rain stops, check your gauge to see how much rain fell. Be sure that your gauge stays level while you read it.

8. On the **Rainfall Chart** (page 25), write the month, the date, and the amount of rain in inches.

9. Empty and dry the jar so that it will be ready for use during the next rain.

10. Repeat steps 6 through 9 four times.

11. Add your measurements together to find the total amount of rainfall during this period of time.

Name _____

Rainfall Chart

Use your **rain gauge** (page 24) to measure the amount of water that falls during five separate rains. Write the dates and measurements on the chart below. Then add these measurements to find the total amount of rain that fell on these five days.

Month	Date	Amount of Rain in Inches
Total		

Name _____

Showers and Flowers

tulip

Warm air and gentle rains make plants grow and flowers bloom. In this way, April showers bring May flowers. Cut these squares apart. Arrange them to make a picture of the special spring flower called a tulip.

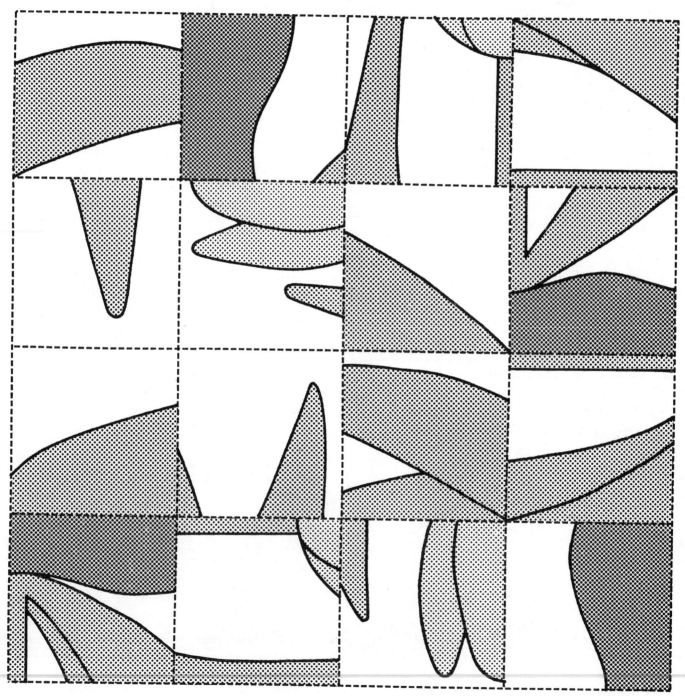

Name _____

Spring Safari

Spring is a time of changes. Take a walk in a field, yard, park, or playground. How many of these signs of spring can you find? Put an **X** in the box beside each one you see.

☐ water flowing in a gutter or storm drain

☐ a puddle left by falling rain or melting snow

☐ an earthworm crawling   or   ☐ a caterpillar eating

☐ animal or tire tracks left in the mud

☐ a bud that is about to open

☐ a spider spinning

a flower that is mostly

☐ red

☐ yellow

☐ blue

☐ a tree or bush with lots of flowers but very few leaves

☐ a branch with new green leaves

Name _____

Rhyme Time

When words begin with different sounds but end with the same sound, we say they **rhyme**. The words *season* and *reason* rhyme. Some words that end with the same letters do not rhyme. The words **pour** and **hour** do not rhyme. Some words that end with different letters do rhyme. The words *flower* and **hour** do rhyme. In each row, circle the one word that rhymes with the first word.

1. bud	rose	mud	bag
2. bloom	book	open	room
3. weather	feather	forecast	water
4. grow	green	snow	how
5. melt	ice	flow	felt
6. cloud	crowd	sky	white
7. shower	pour	flower	slower
8. sun	hot	fan	fun
9. rain	drop	pane	ran
10. thunder	wonder	yonder	wander

Name _____

Spring Fling

Write a poem about spring on the lines below. Use some of the words listed on page 28 in your poem. Make your poem pretty or funny. Draw a picture to go with your poem on a separate sheet of paper. Cut out your poem. Paste your poem and your picture on a larger sheet of paper.

Example

When it rains and showers pour,
I always ask, "Whatever for?"
My mother answers, "For the flowers,"
But I'd prefer some sunny hours!

_____

_____

_____

_____

_____

_____

_____

_____

In Summer

In summer the air is often dry and hot. The sun beats down from a cloudless sky. Roses and daisies bloom. Trees are covered with green leaves. Birds sing, crickets chirp, and locusts hum. Ice cream and chilled lemonade taste good. Summer is the perfect time to go on a picnic, to play in water, or to rest in the shade. Color this picture of summer.

Name _____

Signs of Summer

Take a walk in a field, yard, park, or playground.
How many of these signs of summer can you find? Put
an **X** in the box beside each one you see.

☐ roses in full bloom

☐ grass that is dark green

☐ someone watering a garden or lawn

☐ ants on their way to a picnic

☐ heat making the air above pavement "ripple"

☐ a caterpillar eating a leaf

☐ a ladybug or two

☐ kids playing a game

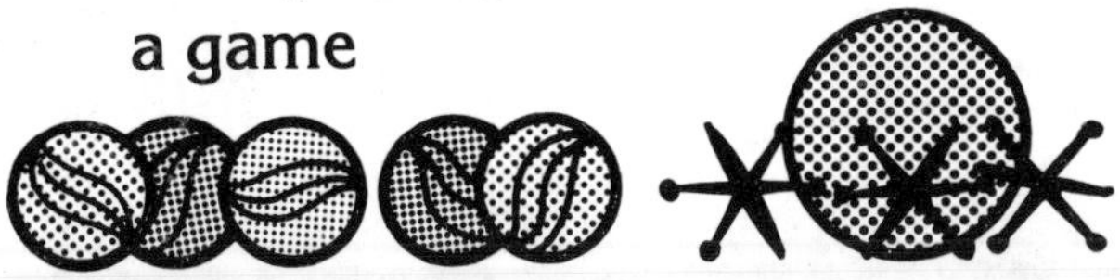

a creature that is mostly

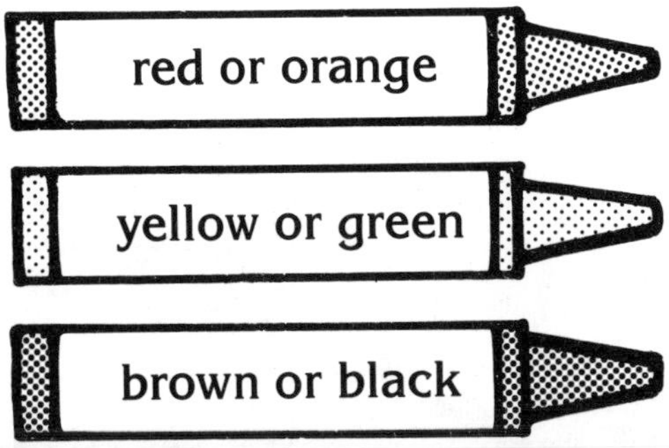

☐ red or orange

☐ yellow or green

☐ brown or black

Name _____

Paste a Picture of Summer

Cut out the squares. Paste each one where it belongs in this picture of summer.

In Fall

In fall the air grows cooler. Sweaters feel good again. Green leaves turn red, orange, or gold. Winds blow them from the trees. Flower petals dry up and drop, leaving seeds behind. Spiders spin their last webs. Some birds fly south for winter. Apples, pumpkins, and nuts grow ripe and ready to eat. Fall is a time of harvest. Another name for fall is **autumn**. Color this picture of autumn.

Name _____

Fall Fun

Fall is a time of changes. Take a walk in a field, yard, park, or playground. How many of these signs of fall can you find? Put an **X** in the box beside each one you see.

☐ flowers that have gone to seed

☐ a pile of bright-colored leaves on the ground

☐ grass that is light brown

☐ a flock of birds in flight

☐ a spider waiting for a meal in its web

a tree with leaves that are mostly

☐ red or orange

☐ yellow or gold

☐ brown or rust

☐ a tree or bush whose branches are bare

☐ a large grasshopper

Name _____

Only Opposites

Opposites are pairs of words that are as different as possible in meaning. For example, the words **high** and **low** are opposites. Draw a line to connect each pair of words that are opposites.

1.	clear	calm
2.	cool	cloudy
3.	dark	cold
4.	day	dry
5.	freeze	fall
6.	hot	light
7.	spring	melt
8.	stormy	night
9.	wet	summer
10.	winter	warm

How Much Do You Remember?

Read these questions carefully. Put an **X** in the box beside each right answer. For some questions, you need to mark more than one box.

1. **What are the four parts of a year called?**
   ☐ days   ☐ months   ☐ seasons   ☐ weeks

2. **Which ones are winter words?**
   ☐ grow   ☐ ice   ☐ snow   ☐ wind

3. **What are tiny pieces of ice called?**
   ☐ cold   ☐ crystals   ☐ cubes   ☐ hard

4. **Which ones are spring words?**
   ☐ bud   ☐ freeze   ☐ melt   ☐ grow

5. **What do we call the way the outside air looks and feels?**
   ☐ breeze   ☐ mist   ☐ warm   ☐ weather

6. **What do we call water falling in drops?**
   ☐ hail   ☐ mud   ☐ rain   ☐ snow

7. **Which word rhymes with thunder?**
   ☐ lightning   ☐ wander   ☐ wonder   ☐ yonder

8. **Cumulonimbus is a kind of what?**
   ☐ cloud   ☐ season   ☐ storm   ☐ thunder

9. **Autumn is another name for which season?**
   ☐ winter   ☐ summer   ☐ spring   ☐ fall

Name _____

Snowman Math

1.

2.

3.

4.

5.

6.

7.

8.

9.

Name _____

Can-Do Clouds

1.

2.

3.

4.

5.

6.

7.

8.

9.

10.

Some Facts About Seasons and Weather

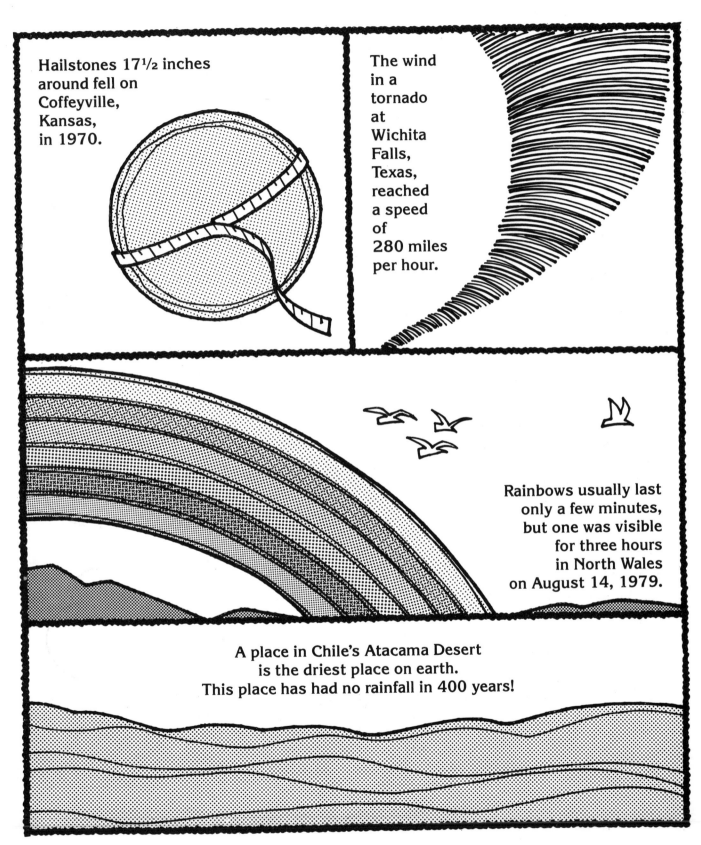

Hailstones 17½ inches around fell on Coffeyville, Kansas, in 1970.

The wind in a tornado at Wichita Falls, Texas, reached a speed of 280 miles per hour.

Rainbows usually last only a few minutes, but one was visible for three hours in North Wales on August 14, 1979.

A place in Chile's Atacama Desert is the driest place on earth. This place has had no rainfall in 400 years!

More Facts About Seasons and Weather

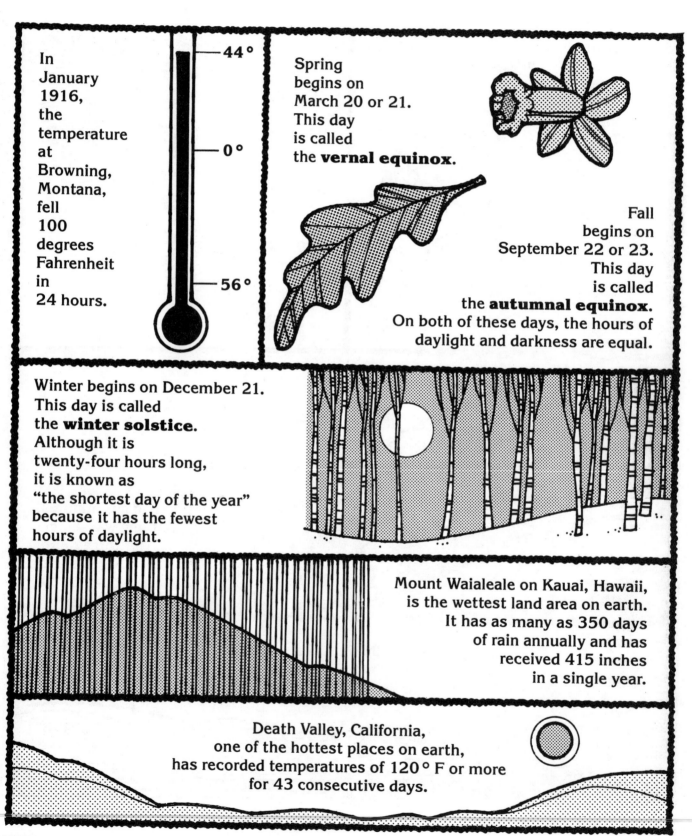

In January 1916, the temperature at Browning, Montana, fell 100 degrees Fahrenheit in 24 hours.

44°
0°
56°

Spring begins on March 20 or 21. This day is called the **vernal equinox.**

Fall begins on September 22 or 23. This day is called the **autumnal equinox.** On both of these days, the hours of daylight and darkness are equal.

Winter begins on December 21. This day is called the **winter solstice.** Although it is twenty-four hours long, it is known as "the shortest day of the year" because it has the fewest hours of daylight.

Mount Waialeale on Kauai, Hawaii, is the wettest land area on earth. It has as many as 350 days of rain annually and has received 415 inches in a single year.

Death Valley, California, one of the hottest places on earth, has recorded temperatures of 120° F or more for 43 consecutive days.

Some Seasonal Terms

altocumulus   Fleecy cloudlets that together look like a group of fluffy cotton balls (page 21).

autumn   Another name for fall (page 33).

autumnal equinox   September 22 or 23, the day on which fall, or autumn, officially begins (page 40).

cirrus   Thin white wispy clouds of ice crystals which form in the cold air high above the earth (pages 20 and 21).

clouds   Visible groups of water drops or ice crystals (pages 20 and 21).

crystals   Tiny pieces of ice that form in the air and may fall to the ground as snowflakes (page 8).

cumulonimbus   A large billowy cloud that is often white on top but gray beneath and may produce severe storms. It is also called a thunderhead (pages 20 and 21).

drizzle   A steady, misty rain of small drops (page 22).

equinox   Either one of two days during the year on which the sun crosses the equator, and the hours of daylight and darkness are equal (page 40).

fall   The season between summer and winter in which some birds fly south, flowers go to seed, the wind blows leaves from trees, and apples and pumpkins ripen (page 33).

gauge   An instrument used for measuring (page 24).

hailstone   A lump of ice that falls from clouds, sometimes during a thunderstorm (page 39).

mist   Tiny droplets of rain that you can see in the air and feel on your face (page 22).

nimbostratus   A cloud that is a dark gray layer of raindrops (pages 20 and 21).

rain   Water falling in drops (page 22).

Some Seasonal Terms
(continued)

season — Any one of the four parts into which a year is divided—spring, summer, fall, or winter (page 5).

shower — A short fall of rain over a small area (page 22).

snowflake — An individual ice crystal. All snowflakes have six points; each snowflake has its own shape (page 9).

solstice — Either one of two days during the year on which the sun is at its greatest distance from the equator, and the hours of daylight and darkness are most unequal (page 40). The summer solstice occurs on June 21 or 22. The date of the winter solstice is December 21.

spring — The season between winter and summer in which days become warmer, trees sprout new leaves, and frequent showers make flowers grow (page 15).

summer — The season between spring and fall in which the air is hot, daisies and roses bloom, the sun beats down, and trees provide welcome shade (page 30).

thunderstorm — A rainstorm in which there is lightning and thunder (page 22).

tornado — A strong, violent whirling wind that looks like a funnel-shaped cloud and sounds like a freight train as it moves over the ground (page 39).

vernal equinox — March 20 or 21, the day on which the sun crosses the equator, and spring officially begins (page 40).

weather — How the outside air looks and feels. Words to describe weather include sunny, partly cloudy, cloudy, rainy, stormy, and windy (page 17).

winter — The season between fall and spring in which days are cold, trees are bare, water freezes, and snow falls (page 6).

_____

has recently completed a unit of study
entitled

Seasons

and is hereby
declared
to be

Seasonally Sensitive

in recognition of this accomplishment.

_____

_____

Special Awards

↑ name tag or note

button

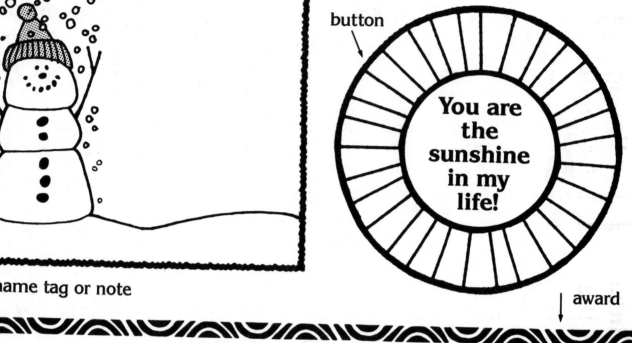

You are the sunshine in my life!

↓ award

Congratulations,

_____ !
(name)

You're a weather-watching wonder.
Nothing escapes your gaze.

_____   _____
(signature)   (date)

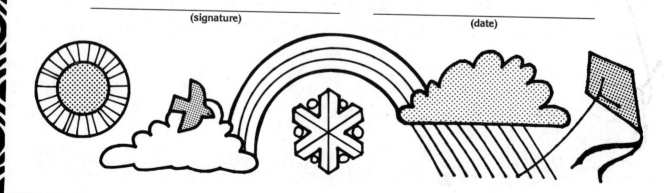

Special Awards
(continued)

Spring into action so you won't fall behind.

Winter is the perfect time to curl up with a good book!

↑ bookmarks

_____ ,
(name)

you are a

_____ *

for all
seasons!

*Add a noun, such as athlete, friend, helper, mathematician, or speller.

Correlated Activities
(for kids to do with adult help)

1. In fall, **deciduous** trees lose their leaves. Depending on the kind of tree, these leaves may be red, orange, yellow, gold, russet, or brown. Collect some of these colorful fallen leaves. Press and dry them carefully between the pages of a book to keep them from curling and fading. Glue them to a cardboard frame to create a leaf wreath for your home or classroom. **(Crafts and Creativity)**

2. Hang a thermometer outside where it is visible through a window but shaded from direct sunlight. Each day for a week, read this thermometer in the early morning, in the middle of the day, and late in the afternoon. Compare these temperatures. Talk about what part of the day is hottest, what part is coldest, and why. **(Observing, Recording, and Comparing)**

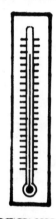

3. Look up and learn the meanings of some of these

Weather Words

barometer	humidity
breeze	hurricane
chinook	meteorologist
climate	monsoon
cloudburst	precipitation
deluge	sleet
downpour	temperature
drought	thermometer
fog	thunderbolt
forecast	twister
gale	typhoon
gust	zephyr

(Developing Vocabulary)

4. Open your local newspaper to the weather page. Find the times of sunrise and sunset. Every Wednesday for a month, write down these times. At the end of the month, decide whether the days are growing longer or shorter. **(Locating and Using Information)**

5. Open your local newspaper to the weather page. Find the reported high temperature and low temperature for your area. Write down these temperatures every day for a week. Use these temperatures to create a line graph. **(Locating and Using Information; Graphing)**

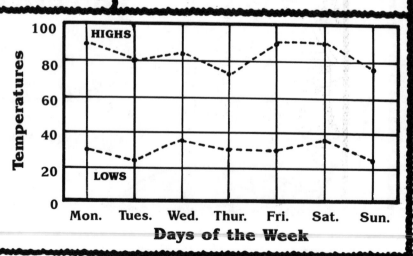

Answer Key

Page 7, Winter Words

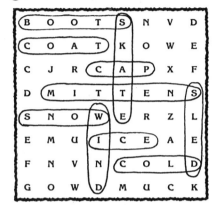

Page 9, Snowflakes

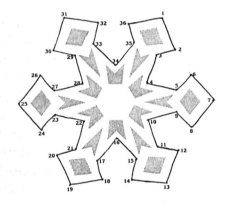

Page 12, Winter Walk

Page 13, All Winter Long

Long vowels appear in the words coat, fire, ice, skate, and snow.

Page 14, Hot or Not?

1. sled
2. coat
3. cold
4. fire
5. freeze
6. ice
7. popcorn
8. snow
9. skate
10. wind

Page 16, Spring Words

Page 22, What Is Rain?

1. shower
2. rain
3. mist
4. drizzle
5. storm

Page 26, Showers and Flowers

Answer Key
(continued)

Page 28, Rhyme Time

1. mud
2. room
3. feather
4. snow
5. felt
6. crowd
7. flower
8. fun
9. pane
10. wonder

Page 32, Paste a Picture of Summer

Page 35, Only Opposites

1. clear–cloudy
2. cool–warm
3. dark–light
4. day–night
5. freeze–melt
6. hot–cold
7. spring–fall
8. stormy–calm
9. wet–dry
10. winter–summer

Page 36, How Much Do You Remember?

1. seasons
2. ice, snow, wind
3. crystals
4. bud, melt, grow
5. weather
6. rain
7. wonder
8. cloud
9. fall

Clip Art